# THE
# GHOST
# TRIO

ALSO BY LINDA BIERDS

# THE
# GHOST
# TRIO

POEMS

BY

# LINDA BIERDS

HENRY HOLT AND COMPANY

NEW YORK

Henry Holt and Company, Inc.
Publishers since 1866
115 West 18th Street
New York, New York 10011

Henry Holt ® is a registered trademark
of Henry Holt and Company, Inc.

Published in Canada by Fitzhenry & Whiteside Ltd.,
195 Allstate Parkway, Markham, Ontario L3R 4T8.

Library of Congress Cataloging-in-Publication Data
Bierds, Linda.
The ghost trio: poems / by Linda Bierds.—1st ed.
p. cm.
I. Title
PS3552.I357G46    1995          94-26063
811'.54—dc20                    CIP

ISBN 0-8050-3485-4
ISBN 0-8050-3486-2 (An Owl Book: pbk.)

Henry Holt books are available for special promotions and
premiums. For details contact: Director, Special Markets.

First Edition—1994

DESIGNED BY LUCY ALBANESE

Printed in the United States of America
All first editions are printed on acid-free paper. ∞

1  3  5  7  9  10  8  6  4  2

1  3  5  7  9  10  8  6  4  2
(pbk.)

*FOR MY MOTHER,*

*Edith Patterson Bierds*

*Grateful acknowledgment is made to the following magazines, where these poems first appeared:*

*The Atlantic Monthly* ("Windows"); *Field* ("It," "Phantom Pain," "Seizure"); *The Journal* ("The Air: Pasteur at Villeneuve l'Etang," "The Bats," "The Iceland Spar," "Lautrec," "Ne Plus Ultra"); *The Kenyon Review* ("Held," "Westray: 1991"); *The Massachusetts Review* ("Hunter"); *The New York Times* ("Care"); *The New Yorker* ("The Fish," "Flood," "Memento of the Hours," "The Reversals," "The Skater: 1775, Susannah Wedgwood at Ten," "Wedgwood: 1790," "The Winter: 1748"); *The Seattle Times* ("Patch").

My gratitude as well to Marian Wood, editor and friend, for her lasting support.

# CONTENTS

## PART III

• *This symbol is used to indicate a space between stanzas of a poem wherever such spaces are lost in pagination.*

# PART I

# THE GHOST TRIO

*1. The Winter: 1748*
   *—Erasmus Darwin, 1731–1802*

A little satin like wind at the door.
My mother slips past in great side hoops,
arced like the ears of elephants—
on her head a goat-white wig,
on her cheek a dollop of mole.

She has entered the evening, and I
her room with its hazel light.
Where her wig had rested is a leather head,
a stand, perfect in its shadow but
carrying in fact, where the face should be,
a swath of door. It cups

in its skull-curved closure
clay hair stays, a pouch of wig talc
that snows at random and lends to the table

a neck-shaped ring.
When I reach inside I am frosted,
my hand like a pond in winter, pale
fingers below of leaves or carp.

I have studied a painting from Holland,
where a village adjourns to a frozen river.

Skaters and sleighs, of course, but
ale tents, the musk of chestnuts,

someone thick on a chair with a lap robe.
I do not know what becomes of them
when the flow revisits. Or why
they have moved from their warm hearthstones
to settle there—except that one step

is a method of gliding,
the self for those moments
weightless and preened as my leather companion.
And I do not know if the fish there
have frozen, or wait in some stasis
like flowers. Perhaps they are stunned
by the strange heaven—dotted with

boot soles and chair legs—
and are slumped on the mud-rich bottom,
waiting through time for a kind of shimmer,
an image perhaps, something
known and familiar, something

rushing above in their own likeness,
silver and blade-thin at the rim of the world.

*2. The Lions: North Staffordshire, 1770*
  *—James Whitfield, 1735–1772*


There are backflows of broom and mayweed,
coal rillets
slick on the mine path.
And the bulrush reeds stretch up from the marsh pond
like the stiffened tails of lions.

I walk toward a village of perfect exchange:
my life taking coal from the earth, then the potter
in turn taking heat from the coal, the earth
giving up an arc shape of pot, and the pot
giving back, in some fired brilliance,
a raspberry vine....

We make from the spines of bulrush reeds
our tallow candles, each turn
in a trough of sheep fat
increasing their marble. They burn with a kind
of spitting and cast to the walls
an equal division of soot and light,

all the surfaces gradually blackening,
around the crucifix, the pastel sketch of
a peach and char.

Through the windows,
great kilns cast the shadows of scent jars.

It is a kind of immortality for us, that entering, that
coming away, icicles thick

in the drift tunnels, our lungs half functioning,
but functioning—each chest with its hissing,
like a room with a brook running under it.

When the earth shudders just over our heads,
we say that the lions are walking,
down from the marsh pond, out through
the seams. We die with their chests
pressed over our chests. In feast position.
In rubble or in bed.

The lions are with us, we say to our children,
although nothing is there but
the bedclothes. They have come for their tails,

that sputter and flare on the bedposts
and mark with their compass-point brilliance
the absolute boundaries of
any world opening under us.

## 3. Wedgwood: 1790
### —Josiah Wedgwood, 1730–1795

When smallpox settles like sand at the knee
each upstep is a rasp, each kneeling
the hiss, then downwash of seedpods.
Just a boy, I limped past a pity
of cantering geese, black-beaked with madness,

each with its burden of drunken rider,
then crossed the short tracks of moorland waste,
the gorse tufts, the low-slung canopies of broom.
Near the treeline, a single deer stepped
into a stillness, watched me from a stillness,
a magical closure of particles, light. Behind me,

the pot banks of Burslem shivered like hives.

I grew, declined. My cane tip
a hail on the cobbles. And each day,
each year, from a salt glaze or green glaze:
knife-hafts, pickle-leaves, then creamers, Queen's ware,
the press of the moulder's board, the dip
of the baller's scale. I visited the chemists.
I visited the soil.

One spring, they severed my leg with a surgeon's blade.

And up through the rice grains of laudanum,
through the stupor, dream, as the blade
wheezed with the breath-strokes of sleepers,
I watched the still globe of our earth

shatter and rush, burst away in an instant—
particles, light. Then a cough. The thin

lispings of thread under skin.
On a wooden limb—brindled and cold as a pike—
I walked and rewalked the kiln-room floors,
saw on the rackworks those jasper bodies, cawk-white
and luminous. And where was I going those years
of my life, pigments of gorse and heath
flaring, fading on the hillsides?

In the royal chambers one morning, I watched
as the Queen, from an elbow pad of claret velvet,
reached up with her forearm and open hand
to the open hand of the glove maker. From her
nails and knuckles to her palm, wrist,
he stroked out a cover of suckling fawn, translucent,

fragile as the inner skin of eggs.
Then a flush rose in the rims of her ears,
as if she imagined an alternate world, as if
through that dappled membrane, she were held
by an alternate world—suspended—like water
by a vase still rich with the coal-scent of fire.
And as long as she did not move at all,
there she would stay.

# MEMENTO OF THE HOURS

First the path stones, then the shadow,
then, in a circuit of gorse and mint,
the room with a brook running under it.
It freshened the milk, the cream that grew
in its flat habit a shallow lacquer,
a veil I tested on slow afternoons
with a speckle of pepper.

There was butter, cheddar, the waxy pleats
of squash, green as a storm pond.
Walnuts. Three families of apple,
each with its circle of core fringe.
And the sheen on the walls
was perpetual, like the sheen
on the human body.

My mother would sit with me there,
her drawstring reticule
convex with scent jars and marzipan, the burled
shapes of the hidden. Once she brought her cut
flowers to chill until evening, and told me
the mouths of the bluebells
gave from their nectar a syrup elixir.

It holds in suspension the voices of choirboys,
she said. A dram of postponement.
And I felt as she spoke their presence
among us: the hum

of the brook just under our feet,
the mineral hush of the plenitude,
then the blackened robes of the blackberry vines
gradually filling the door.

# WINDOWS

When the cow died by the green sapling,
her limp udder splayed on the grass
like something from the sea, we offered
our words in their low calibrations—
which was our fashion—then severed
her horns with a pug-toothed blade
and pounded them out to an amber
transparency, two sheets that became,
in their moth-wing haze, our parlor windows.
They softened our guests with the gauze-light
of the Scriptures, and rendered to us,
on our merriest days, the sensation
of gazing through the feet of a gander.
In time we moved up to the status
of glass—one pane, then two—each
cupping in proof of its purity
a dimple of fault, a form of distortion
enhancing our image. We took the panes
with us from cottage to cottage,
moth-horn and glass, and wedged up
the misfitted gaps with a poultice
of gunny and wax. When woodsmoke
darkened our bricks, we gave
to the windowsills a lacquer
of color—clear blue with a lattice
of yellow: a primary entrance and exit
for light. And often, walking home
from the river and small cheese shop,

we would squint their colors to a sapling
green, and remember the hull
of that early body, the slap of fear
we suffered there, then the little wash
of recovery that is our fashion—how
we stroked to her bones a cadenced droning,
and took back from her absence, our
amber, half-literal method of sight.

# THE REVERSALS

Grit metals drawn to a bourbony syrup,
then the tiny ear trumpet is cast: hand-sized
cornucopia, one tendril of head band.
And the child who has followed this process, pickax
to flame, to the small, curved swelling in his day-pouch,
steps off on a mission to the faltering Beethoven,

just as the other, housebound, in a chaos of music sheets
and chamber pots, steps back through his mind
toward Holland. Late autumn. And by noon,
the ice on the deck rails is a lacework of gull prints.
There are waves, unbroken, rolling port to starboard
like a hammock wind. Deep cold. His hands
are made warm by a wrapping of scarf, his feet

by the black drapery of his mother's lap.
Through his frost-fed and wave-rocked drowse,
three nuns on the deck are a gaggle of sea birds,
the arced wings of their huge headpieces
lifting their slender bodies....

Music sheets. Chamber pots. One beckoning
metronome. And the ear trumpets
send off through his nerves
the sensations of a rake scraped over a harp.`
Great pipe shapes. Ladles. Just a coolness in the palm,
then a warmth. Or lined up on the tabletop,

an orchestra of reversals, sucking sound
back in, bell to a pucker of mouthpiece.

A wind has begun in the clear day.
And perhaps they were spirits, there on the deck boards,
a ghostly trio lifting before him—no land
in sight, then his small body so suddenly
his body, so suddenly *himself,* the hands,
the feet in their soft shoes.

Now a child is standing in the open doorway,
the smallest of ear trumpets shining in his hand:
its perfect walls, the perfect, cupped vessel of it.
Look, he is mouthing, what
has risen from the earth to meet you.

# PHANTOM PAIN

*—Josiah Wedgwood, 1795*


It speaks, now and then.
A lisp at the knee. A needle-trill
where the ankle once arced. Then I reach into air
or the concave disturbance of the bedclothes.

And nothing. A pain in an absence. A leg-shaped
absence in pain. I do not know
what it is that calls—
and burns then, unsummoned, like the summer fires
that flame through the bracken.

A low cloud blackens the larch trees.
We have opened the channel through Harecastle Hill
and the vases and flake-white medallions
float down its dark tunnel, the canal boats
slender as fingerlings. No tow path
exists there and the workers must
leg the boats through: propped on their backs
on the cabin rooftops

must stride down that starless ceiling,
not advancing at all, but
advancing all, walking the eggshell jasper bodies
through the dripping darkness.
They tell me the day draws nearer like a lantern,

as the day must arrive
for the climbing colliers: a whiteness

coming closer—but then, as if on the pond
of the inner eye,

the intricate, inverted brilliance of a maple.
A glimpse into heaven, perhaps, or its loss,
the image flicked upright in the questioning mind—
in an instant, already gone
even as it approaches, a form
flaring nearer while backing away.

# THE SWALLOWS: *1800*

Through the wet and continual trout-chill of earth,
he dropped with his father, past shale beds, black-slush,
down corridors greased with the seeping of springs,
and cranked in the darkness a stuttering flint wheel,
a wand that threw to the pickax and mine walls
quick jitters of light. The sparks left the wheel

in fractured arcs and brought from the darkness
oil slicks, water cans, now and then, a canary
in a wash of anthracite dust, each image
at once arriving, departing, at once

summoned, extinguished. When gasses crept out
through the drift tunnels, the sparks would thicken,
loll at the wheel, flush to the color of rubies, liver,
and be, it seemed, not fire at all, but a wreath
of some alternate element. And before he ran,

pushed by his father—and the other boys
ran with their fathers, calling through the corridors—
he watched at the flint wheel the stopped body
of light, how sparks could be stopped in the shapes
of their bodies, held there, it seemed, forever.

Middays they rested, the axes, the gutteral rasps
of the flint wheels, silent. And his father told him
of legends, once of the swallows of northern nations,
how they gathered by ponds in autumn, joined in a circle

wing to wing, foot to foot, and slowly sank into
the water. How they waited together through winter,

long ice pallets forming above them. And the villagers
stooped on the shoreline, watched through the ice
the chestnut bodies, silent in their still circle.
And waited for spring and the sudden rising,
the small birds breaking together to the yellow day.

But how could they eat there? he asked his father.
And breathe, with the water pressed over them?

They stopped, then began again with their rising.

In a wreath? As a single body they rose?

That is the story, his father said. Though
we think they rose as sparks.

# PART II

# HUNTER

Plume-shaped and pampered, the flames
at the sitting room hearth are the color
of foxes: sharp amber
dropping down to a sobering port.
It is evening. A boy, Charles Darwin,
having listened as the undertaker's workfellows
removed from the sickroom the body of his mother—
a little satin like wind at the door—

turns now to his father's voice.
A story: the magnificent ears of musicians.
The young Beethoven, perhaps. How,
from the blindness of a sleeping mask,
he distinguished for his gathered diners
the clacket of forks from the clacket of knives.

A quick rain has begun at the window.
And now the story veers: an uncle once drowned
in the Derwent River, once walked through a night storm
to the storm of the current. And as the water
rises, as his father's voice
approaches this alternate loss,

Charles studies the flames until they are foxes,
until they are called from the covert,
their sharp scent firm on the kale. Red coats
and the watery breeches. Black boots. And the ears
of the horses are cropped back to walnuts,

nubbled and sore—the long foreheads
just sloping away, sloping,
and the great eyes stark in their sockets.

A music begins then: deep bay
upon deepening bay, the loping hounds
dark and harmonic. . .

And could the uncle distinguish, his father is asking,
the drops of the storm from the drops
of the river? Just then, with his face
half hidden, half blossoming?

And could Charles distinguish, there in the wing chair,
grief from the story of grief? Or fear? Or love
from the story of love? And turn to it—
the grief, the love—harbor it,

however the story might buffer, whatever the loss?
As the man who stands in a yellow field
and takes to his lips a silent whistle,
and accepts that a sound is traveling, just over
the kale, just over the wind, and accepts
his place in some seamless extension,
even as, in a wave, the singing animal world
turns back to him.

# THE WRECKERS: *North Devon, 1842*

They could not affix it, the globe of light
that bobbed on a backdrop of sea.
They could not create from it
a house or steeple, could not fasten it
to any landscape at rest in the chartered darkness.
Then there were two, dipping together,
shifting a little on their short tethers, and surely
they were ships, the nightlamps of
ships anchored at bay.
They set for it then, the inlet, the anchoring,
their cargo of silk, their potatoes and Guernseys,
rum, the bright knuckles of apples
listing as they sailed, then suddenly
lurching—a clapping like whips—
and the beaks of cliff rocks cut up
through the hull, ground up through
the stem and bulwark. There were thieves—
wreckers—dropping in from the cliffsides,
and seawater, fire, the image of crates
passed hand over hand up the dark rocks,
the flags of pale silk lifting through.
And for the swimming crew then, the beach,
and there, in answer to the dipping lights, to
the shattered promise of a harbor:
two horses tethered to an arc
of driftwood, a lantern lashed to each tail.
They grazed side by side through the salt-rich

emptiness. The lanterns bobbed. And the ship,
with an amber outwash of flames, cast
everything back to its origin: green pastures
and the beckoning guidelights of providence.

# NE PLUS ULTRA
*—Thomas Wedgwood, 1771–1805*


## JULY 5, 1805

It nibbles and nibbles, the opium.
A decade. More.
By midday, his lips and eartips are livid, his mind
a lacework stretch that veers with its guide-thread

through a blistering wind. I will journey
to France, he thinks, or Madeira.
To Coleridge. To Jamaica—yes—gather
the larks, the blackwings and thrushes, I
will take their meadow sounds with me.

But sound is a hatchet on tin.
There are workers fixing burlap to his floor, his
wallboards. White runners of cotton
in the windowseams.

There are workers cupping thrushes into cages.


## APRIL 1801

My brother, the headaches subside
and the brief interruptions in sight. Darwin

sends his support for the opium, and Beddoes,
the suggestion to retire with cows.
From the former, something, I think,
in the ecstasy. From the latter, something
in the breath.

I am swept by my theories of light and stasis
and coated a field of white leather
with the crystalline silvers of nitrate. When I cast
upon it the shadow of my hand
the surface darkened with its silhouette!
Magnificent, Jos, my image appearing before me.

Try as I may, I cannot affix it.

MAY 1781

He is watching the bees at the globe
of their hive, their entrances, exits, how they lower
their dead to the chalky ground. Now and then, one
journeys the distance of his hand or elbow, dragging
sensation like a drop of water.
Behind him on the roadway, the potters
cough into their handkerchiefs. He thinks
of the rubicund bodies of his father's kilns.
How a knuckle of mud flares down to a pearl.
All the cameos flawless. Mythic.

## January 1805

I could not affix it. Five fingers
gradually exiting their borders. Or the borders
gradually accepting their backdrop.
And what is perfection? Stasis? Unfadingness?
Some magical closure of particles, light?

I feel that my sisters conspire against me.
Should you dine with them Tuesday or Wednesday,
leave a mark on your outer gatepost.
A scarf or a backstroke of dirt.
A bit of paper on a stick.

## July 9, 1805

It is the day before his death, sunlit, then
sullen, then a sudden rain.
He is stopped in an open carriage, the drops
a shawl across his shoulders, across
the hillsides of thistle and hawkweed.

He resumes when the rain subsides, distracted,
now panicking. The odors of the morning
have magnified, the unbearable grasses,
the unbearable linens and leathers. And the fields
too brilliant, a fiery green. Painful,
they follow him like pain to the hearth,

the bedstead. They follow him into the evening,
a wash of crimson on the footboard, a wash
of green. The rain scent. The leather
just after the rain. I cannot
dismiss it, he whispers, the earth of it.
The colors, odors. The earth of the day.

I cannot advance from it.
Where are my gloves?
What is this permanence I am stopped by?

# AN OLD WOMAN'S MEDITATION

On this northern black morning of winter,
I melt through the pump ice
with a sponge of punk that spits like a toad.
There is snow. Now and then, a shoulder-high
wind. And do not believe that the mind in its age

must through some feebleness turn only backward:
it is the hiss and sizzle of a stubby torch
that renders this memory: September, 1902.
From the grease-wet belly of a fat
locomotive, a single spark jumped into the tinder grass.
Then the fire bred fire. Six hundred thousand acres.
From grass to the waxy salal. From fern
to rooftop to fir to the dozen falls troubling the river,
then jumping the falls, jumping the river, Oregon

to Washington, jumping the lampblack Columbia,
violent updraft winds hurling the burning debris—
its great arc—shoreline to shoreline. I remember
the smoke, a lacework of ash on the wagon,
and then as we left, that airborne arbor,
that arc on the river, some branches in flames,
some branches igniting mid-flight, bursting
mid-flight to their red wings.

In Bridal Veil, a man, then his wife, crept
into the rescue of a mill pond. He with his saddle,

she with a handbag of coral beadwork.
It floated beside her all night like a carp.

A dark water begins now, clears, eats through the snow.
Do not believe that the aged believe. Any more
than the young, the safe. I cannot foretell
my conclusion. Just that, increasingly, my body
is parts: the hand in its dappled glove-work of skin,
the ribcage, the knee. And what of the self,
progenitor of the naming? Perhaps

it is a darkened knuckle of bark, unfolding
to flames at the crossing. More likely a riffle
of snow at some tideline. More likely
some coral-finned fish of the heart.

# THE AIR: *Pasteur at Villeneuve l'Etang*


I am thick on a chair with a lap robe.
Above me, the pines and purple beeches.
Before me, two horses at their hurdles.
They stand and cough and bring with the breeze
the scent of my father's tanning pits:
how the hides, long slumped in the bark-layered graves,
emerged at dusk on my father's arms, pliant
and sheen-cast, like something from the sea.

The horses are bled for diptheria serum
and stand stark-still in their bleeding, like
the horses carved into the chalk hills of England,
the white rivulets of their bones bordered
by rock rose and the slack-lipped vetch.

I believe I am brought here to die. . . .

As a boy I surrendered to chalk, loving
its yellows, its powdered browns. I captured
on paper the rubicund faces of
villagers: a sunken nun, a notary,
the registrar of mortgages, the mayor
of Arbois. Chalk deadens the fingertips
like a fawnskin glove and gives to the air

a seering dust, invisible often, but
thickening. And it is air that offers
the greatest conundrum: freshening while

blackening. Lister writes of the airborne
infections, and Darwin, how the ess-stroke
swimmings of worms aerate the earth—
but bring up to the wind the ribboning poisons.

I have always believed in a vertical purity—

and climbed once, with a rack of sealed flasks
and a mule, the mountains that frame Chamonix.
I proved that our air is crippled with fecundity,
which lessens as we climb, as scent does,
and hue, and the bordering knowledges.

I remember my feet on the glacier,
the crack of steel nippers at the throat of
each vial. How their liquid accepted
a moment of air, before the white flame
of my spirit lamp—its tongue invisible
on the backdrop of snow—closed it all in.

We walked in tandem down the mountain road,
the vials on the back of the mule clicking
and clicking—like willow fronds, I think,
in a smothering ice. And I remember
the reds of the village, how the river
jumped down through the streets. And a choir
of boys in the plaza: sunlight and smoke,
the hide-scent of horses. Someone whispered

the choir notes were purified by bluebells,
a nectar elixir that coated the throat.

And I watched for those moments the wide
sleeves of conundrum: how a quickening liquid
supports a perfection, and the air steps back
from each body in song.

# HELD

Silent, in the loose-fisted grip
of evening, he sits with his infant daughter
and makes from his face an exaggerated mask,
sorrow or glee, shock, the eyebrows launched
toward the hairline, the trenches of the forehead
darkening, so that she might learn—
following, mimicking—not only correspondence,
but a salvaging empathy.

And often in the chambers and drift tunnels
he gestures with the other miners. Deafened
by the strokes of the widow drills, he
offers that mime-talk, clear as the bell codes
for hoist, for lower. Cheeks drawn, the mouth
a tapered egg. Then he turns

in the lamplight, sees the tunnels
gauzed over with dust, feels
his lungs slowly filling, like the gradual
filling of rain ponds, and presses
the widow drill—named for his absence—
through the blue-black petals of anthracite,
through the bones and root tips,
the shale-brindled cradle of the dead
and the flowering, as the earth

of the earth breaks away. Three thousand feet.
Four. His lungs slowly filling. But perhaps I am

spared, he wonders. Perhaps I am held
by this alternate world, cupped

and eternal. As once, just a boy, he stood
with his mother in the bath light.
Her white slip, the twin pallets
of her earrings. A fog of talcum
turned at the mirror. In joy
she delivered its snow to the air,
shake upon shake, smiling,
drawing from his own small mouth
the stunned, obedient smile of a guest.
Her face. Her arm in its little arc.
As if she were saying This
is the gesture for *always* as
the weightless powder settled upon them.

# I T

By wagon, in the first temperate dry-out of summer,
she carried the foxes—their small cages
stacked, cross-stacked, like
the cellular alcoves of hives—
out to the woodland corral, to the fenced run

silver on a backwash of hawthorn.
Then waited as the foxes stepped haltingly out,
to the wood-scent
and the small wind just beginning in the grasses.
In a shallow mote

at the base of the fence line
she had buried an outstretch of
wire mesh. And some nights
watched on a small hillside
as wolves walked out from the hawthorns,

then pranced past the fence posts, all the foxes
moving in waves to the corners,
their silver fur lifting,
opening. The wolves cut
down through the packed soil

and snapped at the wire,
dug to the left, right, a claw
passing through it, a pad,

then barked sometimes like the barking of crows.
And could not understand what it was

that repelled them, what lay between them
and that blossoming world, why
they could not dip down
and resurface: quick sleeve of blackness,
then the salt-rich and shuddering heart.

# THE DEEPS

And we would
go deeper
and cut away
at it, and cut
away at the grave
of it. And deeper,
cutting into the deepest
grave of it,
whatever it
offered, cutting
away. Then each
of us surfaced,
body after body, out
into the day,
like so many
tentative stalks.

# THE PUPPETEERS

With the crimp-slip stitches of netmakers
they have fastened the knee joints, the wrist, elbow,
ankle joints, drawn black-cast fish lines
up to the paddle-bar—from the shoulder, from
the instep, to the calf, through the soft pine swellings
of the thigh. Then watched—son, father—as snow

extended the window ledge, delivered
to the blades of pond skaters
rasps like the strokes of their sanding files.

Then dusk, and the bootprints of the boy
yield a trail to the livetrap, the error
of a porcupine, solitary, attracted by salt
through the closing door. *I will follow another life,*
the child thinks. Away from the calculated glide
or shuffle, the proscenium and leaning-rail,

the string-fed twists, shudderings. Snow, dissolved
by the warmth of the porcupine's back, has refrozen
to a sheath. And the boy—manipulating again
as he has since morning—lifts from his crouching place
in the fir trees a single arm, draws it into the view
of the porcupine: dark sleeve and a red glove,

a little wave, then, in reaction, the slow fan-out
of quills and ice, each tine stretched higher,

drawn higher, single and glistening.
No sounds at all then, no chimney smoke, trees,
the sleeve the whole of the long world—for the animal,
boy—the glove its blood-dollop of sun.

# WESTRAY: *1991*

Then the day passed into the evening,
a sovereign, darkening blue. And
the twenty-six lost miners,
if living at all, knew nothing of the hour:
not the languid canter
of light, or the wind
curled through the hedgerows. Not pain.
Not rage. If living at all then
just this: a worm of black water
at the lower back. At the lungs
two tablets of air.

What is it like there? the broadcaster asked,
his voice and the slow reply
cast down through the time zones of America.

A stillness. All of the families
asleep in the fire station.
And the mineworks pale on the landscape.

What else?
Nothing. Blue lights of police cars.

What else?
Nothing.
Nothing?
...The thrum of the crickets.

A thousand files on a thousand scrapers.
A thousand taut membranes called *mirrors*
amplifying the breed-song. A landscape of cupped wings
amplifying the breed-song. A thousand bodies
summoned to a thousand bodies—and the song itself a body,
so in tune with the dusk's warmth
it slows when a cloud passes over.
Today. Tomorrow. In that May Nova Scotia darkness
when the earth flared and collapsed.
Before that May. After that darkness.
On the larch bud. On the fire station.
On shale and the grind-steps of magma.
On the gold straining in its seam bed.
On the coal straining. On the twenty-six headlamps
swaying through the drift tunnels. On the bud.
On the leaves, on the meadow grass,
on the wickerwork of shrubs:
dark cape of desire.

# PART III

# DESIRE

*1.*

Where the Stillaguamish River cuts down
through the mountains, winds under the summits
of Forgotten and Sperry, of Vesper and Morning Star,

six miners have stepped from their darkened tunnels—
the ore carts stopped on their aerial tramway, the silver
at rest in the spines of railcars. It is a night

of a closer century. Their headlamps dapple
the clearing they cross. Now a robe of bats,
migrating westward, calls them to question
the black sky. And their headlamps lift,
all in one motion, one full beam lighting
the wings, the small, unwavering heads.

*2.*

My father sat in a sunlit chair
and watched the field birds near the Stillaguamish.
He had on his chest, like a bandage, a small
nitroglycerin patch, and on his wrist, like
another bandage, the untanned shadow
of his watch. The birds turned
in the blossoming bulb fields, and Look,
he said, how the leader retrieves them, drawing

them with him in a single stroke, how
the white stomachs flash in unison
as the flock, in unison, rises and dips.


3.


When I was a girl, we followed the river
to its exit in the port, then the port
to the open sea. I would wake with my family
to the sound of two horses, their hoofs on the boardwalk
near our cabin window, and the lumber bolts

clinking like bells. The boardwalk spilled down
to an outsweep of beach, where the horses
were anchored to a purse seine net. I remember
their list as they walked to each other,
dragging the net to its plump conclusion,

all the herring and candlefish, the junk fish,
the wayward salmon, turning together, flashing
together in the early sun. And although

we knew they traveled to us
by a net of our own making,
still we stood spellbound in their unified light.

# FLOOD

In that gill-light of late autumn evenings,
the valley children had crept through the corn rows,
two miles of withering tassels, styles, of leaves
cocked like the flaps of a fool's cap—had crawled
from the gap of the access lane, out
down the rabbit paths, lanky, long-abandoned stalks
the perfect maze. We were parked by the roadside.
Six cars, seven. To the west, the wide
Stillaguamish River swelled to a bay.
Far behind us, the children in the cornfields stood—
no hood, no grit-dusted cap breaching the tassel line—
stepped left, some right—just a ripple, just
a ribbon in the stalks—turned, turned again,
the chirrup of their voices thickening, darkening,
until the quick fear they courted flared and stung
and someone on a step ladder—mother, uncle—
swung a cowbell in a beckoning arc

and homed them all. We were parked by the roadside.
Coffee, the crackle of short-waves. To the west,
the wide Stillaguamish reached over the stop signs,
reached into the eaves of outbuildings, saddles
and private treasures glistening, lifting,
dollops of burlap like jackets in the waves.
On a table-sized island, two Guernseys turned
in a thicket of snowberry, muzzle to tail. As their hoarse
voices collapsed into brays, the wild rain began,
resumed. Water to water. And across the surface

of this new bay, across the pedestal of the rain,
the spawning salmon—steelhead, chinook—having
lost the borders of the river, shuddered and leapt,
thrust in through the mustard fields, through rooftops
and the pivoting sentries of weathercocks, their fins,
the long seams of their bellies stretching, dipping—seeking
one thick current to resist.

# PATCH

On that downslope just over his heart, just
to the right of his left nipple,
on a cream-reach of skin—sometimes warm, cool,
peppered here, then there
with specks the crimson of strawberries—

is a thumb-sized nitroglycerin patch.
It sends to his heart the impulse to open,
to live, to not curl on itself like
a leaf on fire. And it is fire
he remembers now: a forest blazing in acres,

his granduncle, trapped,
rushing ahead toward the wall of the canyon.
How he burned through a fraction of scrubgrass, then
patted it out, stretched his long body
on the blank ashes, drew in his pant legs,

drew in his wide soul, clung
to the blue-black rim of the soil
while the fire jumped over him, slid
with its rattling burn line to the left,
right of him. And although it was just the size

of a shed top, quick breach in a world of burning,
nonetheless the patch held him, the whole of him,
sustained the lifelong expanse of him—balanced
there on a pin-tip of earth, still
rippled with the ghost shapes of grasses.

# SEIZURE

When his eyes took the half-sheened stillness of fish roe,
he tightened his helmet, cinched its inner cap of
canvas straps until the dome above wobbled, swayed
with a life of its own. We were not to touch him,
he said, but wait on the sidewalk until his soul returned.
His hat had a decal that captured light
or hissed out a glow when the light diminished. We were
not to touch him, but watch the ballet of his arcing arm
as he opened the fish, the chum and ponderous king,
flushing the hearts, the acorns of spleen. We were young
together, fourteen or fifteen, and still he returned
to the fish houses, his sharp hands working the knives,
disappearing in flaps of cream-tipped flesh that
closed like a shawl. He showed us the opaque archings
of ribs, brought into our schoolroom the weightless gills,
book-pressed and dried, the spine he had saved that
snapped apart into tiny goblets. We saw him one night
fallen by the river—saw the light from his helmet,
that is, lurching in the long grasses, slicing its
terrible path like a moth grown fat and luminous:
if what flashed there could be seen as a body,
could be stopped in the human hand.

# THE ICELAND SPAR

*"Pasteur liked to look back into the history of things."*
   *—Rene Vallery-Radot*


Then he took in his hand the body
of the crystal, the Iceland spar, as I took

in my mind the body of his movements.
And he walked a little on the woolen rug,

near the windowpane, the damask arcing
of drapes. The spar doubled light into

equal refractions—an achievement unheard of
in the Paris of that year—and gave

to his horse a tandem companion,
to the fruit on his table a plenitude. And to

the milk cart just turning in a banner of sun,
a parallel turning. And surely, he thought,

one image is older—an eye blink, perhaps,
but still, in the wind-hurled journeys of light,

older. And yet captured together in a stretch
of crystal: a magical consort of now and then.

I imagine him cupping the spar down the roadway,
watching the lampposts stretch and double.

•

And the stunned look of a family by the river
as he calls to them waving the blunt baton:

"Let me hold you a moment. No, two. Two!
Let me hold you two moments in the light."

# THE SKATER: *1775, Susannah Wedgwood at Ten*

He would come, Darwin, in a yellow-wheeled chaise,
past the mine shafts and whim gins, the bottle kilns,
past the patchwork of geese on the carriageway,

and counsel her father on the treatment of gums,
of eyelids, or the maddening rasp
in the knee, his long physician's bulk
trembling the floorboards as he walked.

She would stand by his chair
to study his face, his skin with its smallpox scars—
each cupping, she felt, a grain of the finest pepper—
how his chin pulled back as he stammered
his verses: the t's and c's, the shivering n's:

*From Nature's coffins to her cradles turn . . .*

how his fingers resolved into slender tips,
tapered like formal candles.

He brought to her once
two sheep-jaw skates, fearsome and splendid
in their muslin pouch, the teeth in brackets
on the leather boot soles, each jawbone below
filed to a blade. And walked with her then

to the winter pond, the white shrubs
with the blossoms of crows. The teeth were chewed

to a biscuit brown, with streaks of white
where the grasses ran. And the grinding fissures,
spidered like glass, chafed her a bit
when she touched them. *Hang o'er the gliding steel,*

he recited, *and hiss upon the ice. . .*

his words a series of quick clouds
as she circled before him, gliding in fact
on bone, not steel, with the sound of her strokes
less a hiss than a breathing, as if
the lost world resurfaced there.
Dark girl, pushing off with each high-laced boot.
Then the teeth, then the bone, then the mirroring ice.

# THE WHIM GIN

Helmets, flint wheels,
our thick-toed boots, each
with its stubble of coal dust;
the flames of canaries, the lunch tins,
our pickaxes, water cans;
our voices, someone's whistle, inward,
so the lips retreated—everything
piled into whim baskets, raised,
lowered, the horses tight
on a circle above us
pushing the whim beams,
winding the rope that drew us
one after one out into the air
like beads from a sorcerer's mouth;
tight in a circle above us,
unwinding the rope that lowered us,
the whim gin creaking, slipping
a little, the sky a pale plate
of nothingness—nothingness—
then the cirrus-cloud tails
rushing through.

# FROM THE TABLE

Month after dry month. And the sea visited
our lulling hull like a breeze on a hammock.
We were officers, French, pliant and waxed,
adrift in the lounge-rich gap between wars.
I remember our table's damask reach,
the bread plates, the dappled flanks of plums.
And clustered mid-center, to keep us controlled,
to keep us humane, the tokens we mastered:
thumb-sized, bronze, like the stones in some board games,
a gaffe, a ladder, a pebbled wall. We slipped
them between us, before us, whenever
our words bordered on panic, or insult,
or lust, and channeled each other with
a sketch-master's gestures, a hand sliding out
down that glacial linen, another, again,
until at last we were choral and static
and spoke of no issue but the sea—
its lingering star maps—now and then, the heart
of the dark Sargasso. How someone had stopped there,
afloat on that black-weeded, languid pool,
that current-fed magnet to husks and dross,
and watched, drifting in from the south and west,
from seaside houses and wrecked hulls, the storm-torn
trees, the roof beams, and once, the coffin-sized
bob of a child's sleigh. With antlers, he said,
etched into the seat back. Or the remnant strokes
of the child's name. He told us of eels, larval,
transparent, who swim from the weeds to rivers

of Europe, crossing the bars like ice leaves.
Then blooming, taking their bodies and turning,
swimming together in a great wall, back
to the spawn grounds of the black Sargasso.
Thousands of bodies in a great wall.
And the butterflies, he told us, stroking off
from the southern beaches out to the sea.
No nest-land in sight, no thick horizon,
they drop in exhausted clouds of color,
not sinking at first, but afloat, buoyed
by the black grasses. They shatter and fall,
he told us, all in one motion, the way
a rose-stained cathedral window must.
And then they are glass on a darkening glass.
And then they are dust.

# THE BATS: *Beethoven, 1810*

My ears are thick with the matings of drone bees,
their eternal, unvarying thrum.
And with blossoms of swab-cloth that
gradually fill with a yellowing sap. Each dusk
the entire array—earlobes and drones,
the blood-rich canals—is rinsed
with the oil of almonds and a lukewarm
Danube bath. And still

there is nothing. Or a gradual lessening.
Although I have developed a sense
for vibration. This evening I watched
through an open transom
as a gaggle of waiters circled their fingers
on the crystal rims of glasses.
From their postures I knew

they were laughing—washed in white,
with an oblong of Viennese green at their throats.
Each glass supported a measure of water,
then in turn, I assume, a measure
of sound. Somewhat like my bees, but
melodic and choral. I heard nothing directly,

but all in my fashion. That is,
in my ankles and breast. A conversion of sorts,
a form of adaptation, like the darkling bats

who send through the air a method of seeing,
whose voices are eyes and whose ears

translate, like an artist's sketch strokes,
whatever displaces the infinite.
A man, perhaps, his trousers and nightcoat,
his chin line, then the intricate reach

of his skull, each hair stiff
in its singular journey, like the stamen spray
of the night-blooming cereus.

We live as we can. In the eye
of their winnowing paths I am everything.

A man drawn whole by sound.

# LAUTREC

Often I fished with my cormorant, Tom,
who would, through wing dips and shudders, identify
the schools. I remember the knots
on his tepid legs, where skin rippled up from the bone,
and the parallel pickets of his shoulders—
how their pivots found echoes
in my knuckles, when I plucked from the sleeve
a granule of ash.

*The figure is all, and the figure in motion.*

When I opened the fish there were glimmers of
roe, which in turn I turned over
in my study of English: to the deer,
and some dark blemish in mahogany,
in the spill of its quartersawed grain.
How wind through the lips can create such a trio:
fish egg, and doe, and a dapple in wood!

From birth,
my legs held the pliancy of glass.
And shattered, finally, reducing my life to a hobble.
As a boy, rising up from a low chair, I felt
a shin bone buckle and split—a pain,
I assume, like the flare a mollusk must feel, dropped
in the boiling soup. Then the stunned mouth,
all in one motion, closing and opening.

•

As I fell, I saw in the polished grain of the table
the static figure: roe.

When I was insane, I earned my release
with a family of paintings. A circus. From memory.
Demanded from memory. *As if the functioning mind
is one that imagines.* There were gymnasts
and scarves. And once, on their sides
in a center ring, a woman and horse.

They lay facing each other like lovers, or
the twin lobes of the heart. At the sound of a whistle
each would roll over, roll away, the delicate
legs of the horse flailing a little, stroking the air,
the great body below gathering, shifting,
like a galaxy shifts in its black cabin.
Just before they turned over, each
to a separate world, there is a moment
captured in my painting, an instant,

when the shoe of the woman—its cloud of taffeta bow—
reaches out to the answering hoof of the horse.
Her foot—then, in the distance of
reflection, his: as if he, in some fashion,
were her magnificent extension,
and gave to her eyes what my cormorant saw,
as he entered himself in the passing waters.

# CARE: *Emma Wedgwood Darwin, 1874*


With pen nib and glass, on a lozenge-sized leaf,
my husband has counted the two hundred thirty
plum-hued filaments of the sundew plant.

To his left, right, with equal attention,
our sons are sketching each shivering pedicel,
each sap-bloated gland. The coronal splay

of the filaments, their tendrils and curls,
the lateral braids of their journeys,
find echoes—just there on the side tables,

hearth board—in the rims of my father's vases.
We have always visited the soil.
The ink, the marl of it. And made with each piece

a kind of cessation. A pause. Like the moments
one enters in late afternoon, a field perhaps,
or that shadowy climate just west of the door,

when the world's noises suddenly stop—
no leaves, wind, no song birds. That hush,
that instant, before it all rushes on.

The cameo heads are the white of snow drifts.
And delicate, the bridge of a dowager's nose
like a hairline quiver on the inner eye...

•

I remember one March my father,
on a fractured mantle of snow, dragged us
by horseback through the moorland fields, a rope

from the saddle to my cousin's sleigh,
then backward to my brother's, then backward
to mine. Steam bloomed from our various mouths.

And the brittle spindles of new broom, the star-nubs
of heather, the young fern, springing back
through the snow as each rider passed over,

offered the sound of rice paper folding—
or better, unfolding. Two hands releasing
the gift of it. Such concentration. Such care.

# THE FISH

*"...tomorrow I look forward to a greater harvest."*
     *—Charles Darwin, 1832*


Month after dry month, then suddenly
a brief rain has delivered to the fractured hillsides
a haze of grass. So sparse it might be
a figment of the heart. Yet its path
on the outstretched hand is true—brush and retreat—
like the breaths of a spaniel.

There are buried in the decks of certain ships
melon-sized prisms of glass, dangling their apices
to the cabins below. Through
their forked, pyramidic ziggings, daylight
is offered to the mess tables, to the tinware,
the gun-gray curlings of salt-tongue.
Not rainbowed at all, the light
approaches the face of each sailor
in segments, like the light in a spine of
train car windows. Then fuses, of course, when it
marries the retina, its chopped evolution

lost in the stasis of the visible.
We turn homeward soon. I remember
the seam lines of southern constellations, and the twin
tornadoes of a waterspout: one funnel
of wind reaching down from a cloud,
one funnel of sea reaching upward. They met
with the waist of an hourglass—in perfect reflection,

as we, through the Archer, the Scorpion, the Painter,
call forth from the evening some
celestial repetition of our shared churnings.

We shattered the spout
with shotguns that kicked like the guns of my childhood
when leaves were a prune-mulch and my sisters
stood at the rim of the orchard.
Katty. Caroline. Susan. Marianne.
In the temperate wind, their dresses and sashes,
the variegated strands of their hair, were
the nothing of wood smoke. Steam.

I cannot foretell our conclusion.

But once, through a pleat-work of waves,
I watched as a cormorant caught and released
a single fish. Eight times. Trapped and released.
Diving into an absence, the fish
re-entered my vision in segments, arcing
through the pivot of the bird's beak. Magnificent,
I thought, each singular visit, each
chattering half-step from the sea.

# ABOUT THE AUTHOR

Linda Bierds is the author of *Flights of the Harvest-Mare* (1985), *The Stillness, the Dancing* (1988), and *Heart and Perimeter* (1991). The poems in *The Ghost Trio* have appeared in *The Atlantic Monthly, The Journal, The Kenyon Review, The Massachusetts Review, The New York Times, The New Yorker,* and *The Seattle Times.* The recipient of a fellowship from the Ingram Merrill Foundation, Ms. Bierds has also been awarded a National Endowment for the Arts Fellowship in Poetry, an Artist Trust Foundation of Washington Fellowship in Poetry, and a Pushcart Prize, and her work is included in *New American Poets of the '90s.* She lives in Seattle.